To

_____

From

_____

_____

For Mum & Dad, with thanks G.N.
To Freddy and Anna V.T.

BEST LOVED PARABLES
Stories Jesus Told

Text by Lois Rock
Illustrations copyright © 1998 Gail Newey
This edition copyright © 1998 Lion Publishing

The author asserts the moral right to be identified as the author of this work.

First Augsburg Books edition. Originally published as *Best Loved Parables: Stories Jesus Told* copyright © 1998 Lion Publishing plc., Sandy Lane West, Oxford, England.

Library of Congress Cataloging in Publication Data

ISBN 0-8066-3951-2

AF 9-3951

03   02   01   00   99   1   2   3   4   5   6   7   8   9   10

Printed and bound in Spain

Best-Loved Parables
Stories Jesus told

Selected and retold by Lois Rock

Illustrated by Gail Newey

Augsburg
MINNEAPOLIS

Prologue

The person the world knows simply as Jesus was born around two thousand years ago. He lived in a region called Galilee, in the land that is today called Israel.

At that time, the Roman Empire was strong, ruling many countries around the Mediterranean Sea. Among them, Jesus' own country was regarded as a small and rather insignificant province.

Jesus' people, the Jews, remained confident that they were important. In their ancient books, their scriptures, they read of their people's long-cherished faith in God. The one who had made heaven and earth, they believed, took special care of them; one day, a son would be born to them, sent by God to rescue his downtrodden people. He would make God known to everyone in the world.

Was Jesus that special someone? His birth and early life went largely unnoticed, and few suspected that he was particularly remarkable.

When Jesus was a man, however, he lived the life of a wandering preacher, telling people how they could live as friends of God and as neighbors together. As a result, he drew a large following among ordinary people. These people began to ask whether or not he might be the special one sent by God. They gathered in multitudes on the hillsides of Galilee to hear his teaching, to witness his miracles of healing, and to listen to his stories.

These stories—or parables—can be enjoyed as everyday tales of people and the things they do, both wise and foolish.

Yet, for those that long to understand life's mystery, the parables provide a wealth of understanding. The world of Jesus' parables is God's world. By the choices people make, they can live as God's people and make their world part of God's heaven.

Contents

The storyteller on the hillside   6

The mustard seed   8

The yeast   10

The hidden treasure   10

The pearl of great price   11

The tower   12

The rich fool   14

The great feast   16

The lost sheep   20

The lost coin   22

The prodigal son   24

The Pharisee and the tax collector   30

The unforgiving servant   32

The good Samaritan   36

The wise girls and the foolish girls   40

The two sons   42

The sower   44

The story of the sower is explained   46

Epilogue   48

The storyteller on the hillside

Lake Galilee shimmers in the sunshine, a violet amethyst in a setting of low, green hills. Crowds have gathered on a grassy hillside, above the little fishing town of Capernaum.

The people have come to listen to Jesus. Since he moved to Capernaum from the hill town of Nazareth, all kinds of rumors have been flying around. People say he works miracles. Perhaps he is a messenger from God?

Listen: he is speaking right now…

"Look at the birds," he says. (There they are, dipping and curving above the waving grasses, chirruping sunny melodies.) "They do not sow seeds; they do not gather a harvest and put it in barns. Yet your Father in heaven takes care of them. Are you not worth more than the birds?

"And just look at the wild flowers," he continues. It is springtime. The hillside is bright with flax and anemonies, poppies and daisies in shades of pink and mauve, blue and yellow and red. "The flowers do not spin or weave. Yet not even our people's great King Solomon had clothes as fine as the lovely petals they wear. Are you not worth more than flowers?"

Among the crowd are those who can see what Jesus is saying. Surely people are valuable to God, if God fashions flowers with such

love and care—flowers that may bloom only a day before they fade in the sun or are mown down to be burned as fuel. But enough of wondering; listen again to what Jesus is saying:

"So do not worry about money and the things it can buy. Your Father in heaven knows what you need to stay alive. Instead, be concerned above everything else with the Kingdom of God, and living as God wants. God will provide you with all these other things."

From Matthew 6:26–33

The mustard seed

Jesus said, "The Kingdom of heaven is like this:

"A man takes a mustard seed and sows it in his field. It is the tiniest of seeds. Who would ever notice that it had even been planted in the soil?

"Slowly but surely it grows.

"First come the seed leaves; then, more leaves; next, the stem that grows taller... and taller.

"When it grows up, it is the biggest of all plants. It becomes a tall tree, and all the birds come and make their nests in its branches."

From Matthew 13:31–32

The yeast

Jesus told another parable.

"The Kingdom of heaven is like this:

"A woman takes some yeast and mixes it into a great bowlful of flour. The tiny portion of yeast makes the whole batch of dough rise."

From Matthew 13:33

The hidden treasure

"And the Kingdom of heaven is like this:

"A man is digging in a field. As he digs, he comes across a treasure that has been lying there hidden. At once he knows what he must do.

"Excitedly he covers it up again, and hurries off to sell everything he has. Then he returns and buys the field."

From Matthew 13:44

The pearl of great price

"Also, the Kingdom of heaven is like this:

"A man is looking for fine pearls. He loves rich things that are rare and beautiful. He is looking for the perfect treasure.

"One day, he is offered an exceptionally fine pearl. He has never seen one like it. He would give anything to own it.

"And so he goes and sells everything he has. Then he returns and buys the pearl."

From Matthew 13:45–46

The tower

One day, crowds of people were following Jesus. He turned to them and said, "Those of you who want to be my followers must love me more than your dearest family. You must love me more than you love yourself. You must be prepared to face every danger, to carry your own cross like a criminal led out to be crucified.

"Persons who want to build a tower must make their plans carefully. They must work out what the tower will cost, and check that they have enough money to finish the job. If they don't, they may lay the foundation but will not be able to build any more. People will laugh and jeer and say, 'These people started to build a tower but they can't finish the job!'

"In the same way," said Jesus, "you cannot be my followers unless you give up everything you have."

From Luke 14:25–33

The rich fool

"Take care that you do not become greedy in any way," warned Jesus. "A happy life does not consist of having many possessions." And he went on to tell this story:

"There was once a rich man. His land was fertile and bore good crops. As he gazed on his abundant harvest, he began to worry.

" 'I haven't anywhere to store all my crops,' he fretted. 'What can I do? They might get spoiled! Oh, dear, oh dear.' He worried and he worried.

"Then the answer came to him. 'Dear me, the answer's staring me in the face, as plain as can be. I'll tear down my barns and build bigger ones, where I will store all my harvest and everything else I own. Then I will say to myself, "You lucky man. You have all the good things you need for many years. Take life easy. Eat! Drink! Enjoy yourself!" ' How he chuckled with delight at his good fortune.

"But then God spoke to him: 'You fool. You are going to die tonight. Then who will have all the things you have worked so hard to make your own?'

"And that," said Jesus, "is how it is with those who pile up riches for themselves but are not rich in God's sight.

"Do not be afraid. God is pleased to give you the Kingdom. Sell all your belongings and give the money to the poor. Then you will have a purse that never wears out, and you will have your riches in heaven. They will never lose their value, they can never be stolen, and they will be safe from decay. Your heart will always be where your riches are."

From Luke 12:15–21, 32–34

The great feast

One day, when Jesus was a guest at the table of a wealthy man, another guest said to him, "How happy are those who will sit down at the feast in the Kingdom of God."

Jesus replied, "There was once a man who was giving a great feast. He invited a large number of people. When it was time for the feast, he sent his servant out with a message for the guests: 'Come! The preparations have been made. Everything is ready.'

"One by one, they all began to make excuses.

"The first one said, 'I have bought a field, and must go and look at it. Please tell your master how sorry I am.'

"Another said, 'I have bought five pairs of oxen and am on my way to try them out; please tell your master how very sorry I am.'

"Another one said, 'I have just got married. For that reason, I cannot come. Please tell your master how truly sorry I am.'

"The servant went back and told his master the news. The man was furious.

"He sent his servant out on a new errand. 'Hurry out into the streets and the alleys of the town,' he ordered, 'and bring back the poor, the crippled, the blind, and the lame.'

"The servant swiftly did as he was told, and then returned. 'Sir,' he said, 'your order has been carried out, but there is still room for more.'

"So the master said to the servant, 'Go out to the country roads and lanes and make people come in. I want my house to be full. But I tell you: those who were first invited but did not come will not taste the dinner.' "

From Luke 14:15–24

The lost sheep

One day, when many outcasts and people of low repute came to listen to Jesus, the religious leaders started grumbling, "This man welcomes outcasts and even eats with them!" How they muttered. How they all frowned.

They believed they knew all about God. They believed that to eat with a wrongdoer was in itself to do wrong. So they wondered how Jesus could claim to know about God. Jesus told them this parable:

"Suppose one of you has a hundred sheep. You notice that one is lost. What do you do?

"You leave the other ninety-nine grazing safely in the pasture, and go looking for the one that is lost.

"You look and you look. You do not stop looking until you have found your missing sheep.

"When you find it, you are delighted. Gently you pick it up, lay it on your shoulders and carry it home.

"Then you call out to your friends and neighbors, 'Listen, this is a happy day for me! I lost one of my sheep, and I have found it again. Let us celebrate!'

"In the same way, I tell you, there will be more joy in heaven over one sinner who repents than over ninety-nine respectable people who do not think they need to repent."

From Luke 15:1–7

The lost coin

"Think of a woman who has ten coins," said Jesus.

Many of the women who were listening had a headband jingling with ten coins. It was part of the traditional wedding gifts—valuable in itself, and a treasured reminder of the beginning of their grown-up lives.

"One day," said Jesus, "the woman in my story loses one of her special coins. What does she do?"

"She gets right down on her hands and knees and she starts to look for it," called someone from the crowd.

"So she does," agreed Jesus. "She lights a lamp and sweeps her house. She looks high and low for her precious coin until she finds it.

"When she finds it, she calls her friends and neighbors together and says, 'Listen, this is a happy day for me. I lost one of my coins, and I have found it again. Let us celebrate!'

"In the same way, I tell you, the angels of God rejoice over one sinner who repents."

From Luke 15:8–10

The prodigal son

Jesus told yet another story about being lost and being found:

"There was once a man who had two sons. One day, the younger one came up to him with a harsh demand: 'Father, when you die, part of your property will be mine. I want it *now!*' The son's face was set in a cold and bitter expression. How he hated being at home.

"The father agreed to the young man's request, although he was deeply saddened at being treated in this way. Within a few days the son had sold his share and left home with a great deal of money.

"He traveled to a far country. Good times beckoned, and he spent the money lavishly on luxuries and wild living.

"Then, famine struck. In no time at all, the young man found that all his money had gone. He had frittered it all away!

"Desperate and starving, he went looking for work. Times

were hard. The only job he could find was looking after a herd of pigs. There, in the dust, he watched the pigs rooting hungrily at their feed of bean pods, and wished that he could eat their food… for he had nothing to eat—nothing at all.

"At last he came to his senses. 'My father's servants live better than this,' he said. 'They have more than they can eat, yet here am I about to starve. I will go back to my father and tell him how sorry I am. "Father," I will say, "I have sinned against God and against you. I am no longer fit to be called your son. Please treat me as one of your servants." '

"Then he set out on the long journey home.

"While he was still a long way from home, his father saw him coming, and his heart was filled with pity. He ran to meet his son, threw his arms around him and kissed him.

" 'Father,' said the son, 'I have sinned against God and against you. I am no longer fit to be called your son.'

"But the father took no notice. He called to his servants. 'Hurry!' he said. 'Bring a fine set of clothes and put it on my son. Put a ring on his finger and shoes on his feet. Then let us take a fine, fat calf and celebrate with a feast! For this son of mine was dead, but now he is alive again. He was lost, but now he has been found.'

"And so the feasting began.

"Meanwhile, the elder son was out in the fields, working. As he came back to the house, he heard music and dancing. Puzzled, he asked one of the servants what was going on.

" 'Your brother has come back home,' the servant answered. 'Your father has taken a fine, fat calf and is giving a party to celebrate—he is so glad your brother is back safe and sound.'

"The elder brother was livid with rage. He was so angry he would not even come into the house. His father, dismayed, came and pleaded with him.

"The elder brother turned on him in fury: 'All these years I have worked for you like a slave, and I have never disobeyed you. What have you ever given me? You haven't even offered me a goat for me to have a feast with my friends. But this young son of yours wasted his money in wild living, and when he comes back, you take the very best calf and give him a splendid party!'

" 'My son,' replied the father, 'you are always here with me and everything I have is yours. We had to celebrate and be happy, because your brother was dead, but now he is alive; he was lost, but now he has been found.' "

From Luke 15:11–32

The Pharisee and the tax collector

Jesus told this parable to people who were sure of their own goodness but despised everyone else:

"Once there were two men who went up to the Temple to pray. One was a Pharisee— a very religious man, who knew the scriptures and, from them, the laws that tell us how to live as God's people.

"The other was a tax collector. He gathered money for the Romans who rule our land, and took more than a little extra for himself.

"The Pharisee walked up confidently and stood proudly in a space by himself. 'I thank you, God,' he said, 'that I am not greedy or dishonest, or someone who cheats even his own wife, as other people do. I thank you that I am not like that tax collector over there. I fast two days a week, and I give you a tenth of all my income.'

"The tax collector stood further back and would not even lift his face to heaven. He hunched over sorrowfully and said, 'God, have pity on me, a sinner.'

"I tell you," said Jesus, "it was the tax collector and not the Pharisee who went home with his friendship with God mended. For everyone who thinks they are someone great will be humbled; everyone who sees that they cannot claim greatness in God's eyes will be made great."

From Luke 18:9–14

The unforgiving servant

Peter was one of Jesus' closest friends. One day, he came to Jesus with a question: "Lord, if my brother does me wrong, how many times do I have to forgive him? As many as seven times, perhaps?"

"No, not seven times," said Jesus. "You must forgive him seventy times seven, because the Kingdom of heaven is like this:

"There was once a king who decided to check how much each of his servants owed him. He had just begun to do so when one was brought in who owed him millions of dollars.

"The servant did not have enough money to pay the debt, so the king ordered that he be sold as a slave, along with his wife and children, in order to raise the money.

"The servant fell to his knees. 'Please be patient with me,' he begged. 'I will pay you everything.' The king felt sorry for him, so he forgave him all the debt and let him go.

"Then the man went out and found one of his fellow-servants—one who owed him just a few dollars.

"He grabbed the poor man by the neck and started choking him. 'Pay back what you owe me!' he demanded, menacingly.

"The servant fell to his knees. 'Please be patient with me,' he begged. 'I will pay you everything.'

"But the first servant refused to wait. Instead, he had him thrown into jail, warning that he would never allow him to be set free until he had paid back everything.

"When the other servants saw what had happened, they were dismayed at such injustice. They went to the king and told him everything.

"The king called the first servant in to him. 'You worthless slave!' he rebuked him. 'I forgave you the whole amount you owed me, just because you asked me to. You should have had mercy on your fellow-servant, just as I had mercy on you.'

"The king was very angry, and he sent the servant to jail, warning him that he would never allow him to be set free until he had paid back everything."

Jesus added, "That is how your Father in heaven will treat every one of you unless you forgive your brother from your heart."

From Matthew 18:21–35

The good Samaritan

One day, a teacher of God's law came up to Jesus. He wanted to trap him with a clever question that Jesus wouldn't be able to answer. "Teacher," he asked, "what must I do to receive eternal life?"

Jesus asked him, "What do the scriptures say? How do you explain what you read in them?"

The man quoted the ancient writings of the Jewish people: " 'Love the Lord your God with all your heart, with all your soul, with all your strength, and with all your mind' and 'Love your neighbor as you love yourself.' "

"You are right," said Jesus. "Do this, and you will live."

But the man was annoyed that Jesus had dealt with his question so cleverly and so quickly. So he asked another question: "Who is my neighbor?"

Jesus answered with a story:

"There was once a man who was traveling down the road from Jerusalem to Jericho. There, in a lonely spot, robbers attacked him, stripped him and beat him up, leaving him half-dead.

"It so happened that a priest, who led the worship of God in the Temple in Jerusalem, was going down that road. When he saw the man, he walked by on the other side of the road.

"Then a Levite came, an assistant in the very same Temple. He went up to the man and looked at him. Then he, too, walked by on the other side.

"Finally a Samaritan came along.'

Jesus paused for a moment. His listeners were left wondering, "Why has he chosen to bring a Samaritan into his story? Our people despise the Samaritans! They do not respect our Temple in Jerusalem as they should—and that is clear evidence that they don't worship God in the right way!"

Jesus continued the story: "When the Samaritan saw the injured man, he was filled with pity for him. He went over to him, poured oil and wine on his wounds, and bandaged them. Then he lifted the man onto his donkey and took him to an inn, where he took care of him.

"The next day he took out two silver coins and gave them to the innkeeper. 'Take care of him,' he told the innkeeper. 'When I return this way, I will pay you whatever else you spend on him.' "

Then Jesus asked, "In your opinion, which one of these three acted like a neighbor towards the man attacked by the robbers?"

The teacher of the Law answered, "The one who was kind to him."

Jesus replied, "You go, then, and do likewise."

From Luke 10:25–37

The wise girls and the foolish girls

"Always live your life so you can give an account of your actions without feeling ashamed," warned Jesus. "You do not know the time when you will have to give an account of your life. When the time comes for you to do so, the Kingdom of heaven will be like this:

"Once, ten girls were excitedly getting busy for a wedding celebration. Their job was to welcome the bridegroom when he arrived to claim his bride. They took their oil lamps and went out to wait for him.

"Five were wise. They took extra oil with them.

"Five were foolish. They had only the oil that was already in their lamps.

"The bridegroom was late, and the girls yawned as they grew sleepier and sleepier. Finally, they all fell asleep.

"It was midnight when the cry rang out: 'Here is the bridegroom! Come and meet him!'

"The ten girls woke up with a start and trimmed their lamps to make them burn more brightly. Then the foolish girls noticed that their lamps were dim. 'Please let us have some of your oil,' they said to the others.

'Our lamps are going out.'

" 'No indeed,' replied the wise girls. 'There is not enough for your lamps and ours as well. You must go and buy more oil.'

"The foolish girls hurried off. While they were gone, the bridegroom arrived. The five girls who were ready went in with him to the wedding feast.

"Later, the other girls arrived. 'Let us in,' they pleaded. 'Certainly not,' replied the bridegroom. 'I don't know who you are.'

"So always be on your guard," warned Jesus.

From Matthew 25:1–13

The two sons

Some of the chief priests were arguing with Jesus. "What right have you to be telling people about God?" they complained. "Who gave you this right? You haven't studied to be a religious leader!"

Jesus did not answer them directly. Instead, he told them a story:

"There was once a man who had two sons. He went to the elder one and said, 'Son, I want you to go and work in the vineyard today.'

" 'I don't want to go,' the young man answered, sulkily.

"However, as the day wore on, the son remembered how the grapes were growing in the sun. He thought of all the work that needed to be done so that the whole household could enjoy a good harvest. Without further ado, he went off to the vineyard.

"The father also went to his other son, and asked him to go and work in vineyard.

" 'Of course, Father,' replied the young man politely; but he didn't mean what he said. His mind was on other things, and he didn't want to work to be sure of a good harvest. So he didn't go.

"Now tell me," said Jesus, "which of the two actually did what their father wanted?"

"The elder one," answered the priests. There was no other answer that made sense.

"Quite so," said Jesus. "And I tell you this: some of the people who have lived wicked and scandalous lives will be going into God's Kingdom ahead of you. For they have listened to the warnings to change their ways and live for God. But, even when you saw this happen, you did not change your minds and heed the warnings."

From Matthew 21:23, 28–32

The sower

There, where the farmlands reached down to the shore, crowds of country people had gathered to hear Jesus. He told them this story:

"Once there was a man who went out to sow grain. He scattered seeds from the basket that was slung from his side. As he threw the seed, some of it fell along the path, where wild birds swooped down and ate it.

"Some fell on rocky ground, where the soil was thin. The seeds soon sprouted in the crumbly soil. Then the sun came up, bright and scorching. The young plants shriveled in the heat, for their roots did

not go down deep enough, and they died for lack of water.

"Some of the seed fell among thorn bushes. The wild thorns grew quickly and choked the seedlings.

"But some seeds fell in the good earth of the field. They produced strong plants, each with a full ear of corn. Some ears had a hundred grains; others sixty, and others thirty."

And Jesus ended his story with these words: "Listen, if you have ears to hear the message of the story."

From Matthew 13:1–9

The story of the sower is explained

Jesus' disciples were confused. "Why do you always talk in parables?" they asked.

Jesus replied, "Only some people can understand the message about God's Kingdom. The rest hear the story, but they do not know what it really means. You are fortunate, because your eyes see what is true and your ears hear the message.

"Listen, then, to the meaning of the parable of the sower:

"Those who hear the message about the Kingdom but do not understand it are like the seeds that fell on the path. The Evil One swoops down and snatches away their understanding of what it says about God before it can take root in their minds.

"The seeds that fell on rocky ground are like the people who hear the story's message and are at once excited to be part of God's Kingdom. But their enthusiasm does not last long. As soon as trouble comes, they give up.

"The seeds that fell among the thorn bushes are those who hear the message and understand what it means. But then they let the worries of everyday life take all their time… and they never get around to doing anything for God's Kingdom.

"The seeds that fell in good soil are the people who hear the message and understand it. They change the way they live their lives and they bear a rich harvest for God's Kingdom."

From Matthew 13:10–23

Epilogue

Jesus worked among his people, healing, preaching, and teaching, for three years. By then, he was a man with a price on his head, wanted by the religious leaders of his own people. They felt deeply threatened by his easy confidence in talking about God, and his message of love and forgiveness. They became his bitter enemies, and they arranged for Jesus to be put to death as a criminal.

It seemed like the end; but three days after Jesus' body was laid in a stone tomb, his friends claimed that they had seen him. They said he was alive in a new way that death could never conquer. Bravely they spread their message throughout the world. They said that Jesus was God's promised one—the Messiah, the Christ. They said that the message of his life and his stories pointed the way to a life of love, of joy, and of peace with oneself and with one's neighbors.

Most of all, they said, he showed the way to peace with God, and to a friendship with God that death could never end.